SUCCESS
IS A WAY OF
LIFE

CHRISTOPHER HILLS

Editor
Ann Ray

MICROALGAE INTERNATIONAL SALES CORPORATION
Boulder Creek, CA 95006

Printed in the United States of America.

Library of Congress Cataloging in Publication Data

Hills, Christopher B.
    Success is a way of life.

    1. Success.   2. Ray, Ann, 1937–   II. Title.
BJ1611.2.H55   1983   158'.1   83–19417

ISBN 0–916438–49–X

TABLE OF CONTENTS

INTRODUCTION

It is often with some surprise that people discover that success is really all about self-mastery. We are our own worst enemies, and getting control of ourself and our emotions is the ultimate success for all of us.

The chapters of this book were selected by the editor from talks that I gave over a period of years, so at times you may find the "spoken" quality in the wording, rather than the "written." The attitudes and laws of life in each chapter are simple, and it is best to read a little at a time and ponder it, rather than speed quickly through the book. If you actually apply what I have recommended, success will begin to blossom in many areas of your life, for real success begins at the deeper levels of who we are and how we interact with people.

You leave your mark on history by the depth of your relationship with people, not by the amount of your possessions or money. But if you have great wealth and can forge deep relationships too, you can enrich the lives of many people all over the world.

The riches of the soul described in this book, however, refer to the kind of success which will enrich the soul of mankind for eternity. Only self-mastery can achieve this.

Christopher Hills
July, 1983   Boulder Creek, CA

SUCCESS IS A WAY OF LIFE

If you asked any great man or woman the secret of success, I am sure you would get different answers. One would say perspiration instead of inspiration; another would say the power of imagination which lights up the mind. Another would say self-discipline, and yet another would say the power of positive thinking or faith.

Admittedly all our heroes would agree that without a sense of conviction about where they were going, they would never feel the driving force of emotion and self-determination which saturates the lives of all supremely great achievers.

But success cannot be measured in setting records or achieving wealth or in human ingenuity. Many heroes die a grisly death and many great achievers reach their goals at the expense of their happiness. Nikola Tesla, the genius inventor of countless electrical devices including the A.C. motor, died in abject misery and was penniless. Even Christ was brutally tortured and then crucified among thieves. Receiving a common and painful death given to wrongdoers in Roman times in exchange for a life of selfless service, is not our idea of social justice. Yet many of our famous achievers have risked their own lives and personal happiness in order to make others happy or give something they believed in to the world. The Spartans who defended the pass at Thermopylae against the millions of Persian troops would rather have died than give in to failure and lose the battle. The very teaching of Christ says those who can stay with it to the end shall inherit eternal life and happiness.

But how to stay the distance? How to go through the flogging and the crucifixion, and how to keep the spirit up when all around us is dark and sickening?

This is the secret quality that transcends all circumstances and conquers the despair that overtakes even the supremely great. How do they do it and still call forth the love and wisdom that lies hidden deep within us?

The answer that comes over and over again to me is in the word enthusiasm. Without enthusiasm you cannot go on trying and trying. Without enthusiasm you cannot face the dark future. Without enthusiasm for reaching eternity or giving us the kingdom of happiness, there would be no Christian religion today. And without enthusiasm for truth, there would be no science.

So what is enthusiasm and how do we get it? The word means "filled with inspiration" or filled with spirit. The Greeks invented the word because they believed people who had it were possessed by the gods; they had some extra ability to become filled with the power to do the impossible.

But all great people have said the same things about this one quality which they all had in common. Whether they believed it came from God or whether they were able to wake it up in themselves makes no difference. All of them had the power to summon up the inspiration or spirit whenever they needed that extra burst of energy, faith or love. They all said the same thing about enthusiasm—that it came from within and yet it was available everywhere and existed in everybody.

That is the secret! To know that you don't have to believe in any particular gods, religions or philosophy in order to get it. It was available in ancient Greece to the great athletes as well as to the great poets and sculptors. It was available in ancient China to the painstaking astronomers as much as to their masters of wisdom. Lao Tse called it mysterious, unfathomable, but incredibly great and subtly powerful. The Muslim cry is that God is great. Einstein saw it as so infinite and vast and intelligent that even to think of it was awesome and humiliating. Even the idea of a hero is someone who has the humility to use this power to do the impossible.

But how can you tap the never-ending Source of this intelligence or great spirit unless you believe, or have some sense of conviction, that it can fill you with enthusiasm and power to go tirelessly on and on?

Such is the power of endless enthusiasm because all other qualities of human endurance, perspiration, self-discipline or faith ultimately spring from the ability to endure to the end. Suicide is the abandonment of that hope, and failure is the abandonment of that spirit.

For to the great, failure does not exist. Each failure is just another lesson in a great and mysterious spirit working through evolution. The great evolutionary intelligence itself, which gives us our brains, our genes, our bodies, has made all its mistakes into successes, all its millions of failed sperms and eggs and seeds into the triumph of the one seed that germinates. Fertilize one egg and it will produce hundreds more which can be destroyed over and over without affecting its power to reproduce itself.

The universe bestows this power on anyone who can lift their mind and consciousness up into the realm of enthusiasm, for this one quality is infectious to others. If even one cell of our body can be saturated with the spirit, it can intoxicate all others around it.

If you find even one cell of your body which can send out the signal of enthusiasm, you can be a success. For success does not depend on money or fame or name but on your ability to summon up bliss in the midst of pain, to know love in a world that is seething with hate. Success is joy and laughter and lightness of heart in the midst of heavy burdens. Success is the ability to carry the world's problems on your back and yet feel that the yoke is easy and the burden is light.

For with the spirit of life bubbling within you, how can you ever fail? The successful can destroy everything they have ever built or done and start again. For the truly successful have discovered a secret. Life is not books and scriptures and traditions, but the way you live.

Look into your soul now and look at the way you live and measure your self-image by the love you share. The fire of enthusiasm you have for life is the measure of your success; for success is a way of life.

TAKING CONTROL OF YOUR LIFE

How many people actually use their consciousness in such a way that they are fully aware of everything that has to be done at every moment, rather than letting the situation dictate what has to be done? How many people live a life that is governed entirely by what happens to them, instead of them happening to the world? How many people are able to think ahead and anticipate before something happens, rather than just react to a person or a need or to some situation that arises? How many people allow things to happen to them and then decide how they are going to respond or what they are going to think, instead of *making* everything happen by being aware of what lies in their unconscious desire that leads them secretly into everything they are experiencing?

If someone or some situation is making us unhappy or we feel disturbed by the world situation, how much are we ourselves responsible for that disturbance? We might "think" it is the others' actions towards us or we think evil people can disturb our peace, but this is true only if we allow them to affect us. If we allow that, then they can control us, manipulate our feelings, make us miserable. The skillful way of living is to remove the cause of the obstruction, to remove that which prevents our will from manifesting its desire. The problem is that our real desire is often unconscious and unknown to us.

If we could understand our *will* and how it works, our unconscious mind could not control our destiny. What is will? The word comes from an Old English word, "wille," meaning "desire." So will is desire, the secret desire that is in the unconscious. It sits in the heart, as it were, and creates our interest in life. When we have the will to do something, we have an interest in doing it; when we don't have any will, it is because we're not turned on. So will is really a condition of the heart, and when we come to do some work and we have no will to work, or when we come to do some changes on ourselves and we have no desire to change, then there is a conflict between our unconscious and our conscious mind. Your conscious mind might say, "I want to communicate well," but then you just mumble something between your teeth. In your mind you think you've communicated, but everyone says, "I didn't hear you," or "You were just talking; I didn't really know you meant that." You think you've communicated but because you are in conflict, there's something that holds you back from coming out and saying in a way that really hits home, "Look man, I'm talking to you. Wake up. Listen, I'm really saying something." Instead, you just mutter and expect the person on the other end of the mutter to do all the work.

We're all lazy that way. Why are we lazy? Because we are frightened to make a great effort to communicate, to really say that we've said something. So what happens to us? We find that people misunderstand us. People don't get the message, because we don't have any will behind what we're saying. We don't have the force of the heart, or the desire. If we really had it, we would make the *effort* to communicate, just like we make the effort to get up at four o'clock in the morning to go fishing. If we really like to go fight fires to be a hero, or whatever, we will get up in the middle of the night when that siren goes off, and think nothing of it, because we have that will to do it.

Now who else wants to do that? We're so glad that there are such people around to make all that effort to be heroes. They have the will, the desire, to do it. And it is the same when people have a hobby; they will do an enormous amount of work, running here and there, spending thousands of dollars on boats and fishing gear and bows and arrows as long as they want to do it. Ten thousand dollars on a camper or on equipment. When we want it, we've got the money.

When you have the will, that's because the heart is saying, "I've got to have it, whatever it costs." When that energy is behind whatever you're doing, you get it. That's what often gets you into trouble, too, isn't it?

When you get the camper, you've got to make the payments. People who are in that state of consciousness don't think about the payments until they've lost their job or something like that. Their whole life becomes working to meet payments, and they can't see that they got themselves into that situation by desiring it so much. Then, when their life is a wreck, they think, "My debts are up to here, my life is a mess, I've got to get out, commit suicide or something. Not that I'll *change*; I'll just get out of it. Go bankrupt, of course, that's the answer."

They don't see that their unconscious desire brought them into that situation. In the spiritual life, Christ says that unless you can put all your consciousness and all your interest and all your will into what you are doing, you'll not succeed. This was his teaching: "Love thy God with all thy heart and all thy might and all thy soul and all thy mind," with everything you've got, otherwise it's not going to work. In other words, put all your consciousness, all your attention, on what you're doing.

This is a very simple law, isn't it? We do it quite easily when there are other things we want to do, like buying a new car; we put all our consciousness on that very quickly. Or falling in love with somebody. Nice groovy person over there and we say, "Gosh, I'd like that one for me," and we start pulling all the strings and doing all the tricks of the trade that are going to get that one for me. Right? Smiling, dressing up, and lipstick, and telephoning, and getting to know, and making all the opening gambits and things, to get that one, but we don't make those efforts for our spiritual life. We only go there when we are pushed, when the situation is so rotten and so bad that we've got to make a move, we've got to make a change, because we cannot go on any longer with that pain. But our will is not in it, so there's always this conflict between the heart or the will and what is in our imagination. In our imagination we think of ourselves as great beings, maybe gurus or something much greater than we probably are. We believe, in our imagination, that we deserve all the things we dream about. And so we try to get those things, whether it's power—dreaming of ourselves as kings and queens, politicians, presidents—or lovers, or whatever.

Christ is saying that we will attract everything that is good for us, the abundant life, if only we can get our unconscious clear so that it is not running our life but we are running it. In other words, we must have mastery over what is lying deep in ourselves so that we are not just being swept along from one situation to the next but can actually create the situations and not allow the situations to create us. Christ surrendered to God's will because he saw that cosmic laws could bring heaven on earth and he wanted that so much, he could easily give up his own personal decision-making power to that power which governs the totality of life. He saw clearly that we don't have to make decisions from pressures from this person and that situation but we actually can make the choices and decisions ahead of time so that all things happen according to how our being is. Even if something totally unexpected happens to us, it is the state of our being which determines how we shall react to that situation.

Acting according to our true being means that we are acting in concert with the will of the universe; there is no separation between what the universe wants and what we want, no conflict between the imagination and the will, no struggle between the head and the heart. This is why Christ said that all you have to do is put everything you've got on the one thing and then, if you deserve the other things, you will get them. When you are acting from true being, you will be very desirable to many people, so instead of having to run here and there after various human personalities, the one you are running after notices that light in you and sees that is something he or she wants and so there is irresistible attraction. You don't have to worry about getting what you want, because if you've got that light, you will attract good fortune. Angels will watch over you and even work for you to bring about the impossible. When you have the light of the spirit within you, there is always enthusiasm because you are in love with life. However hard the task becomes, the difficulties melt away in the fire of the spirit. When you have that fire, you fall in love with love itself and know that life is born and reborn through love.

There are some who come up to me after a talk or seminar and ask if I have been born again. I smile inside because they don't understand that a person who is in love with all life is not only twice born but thrice born. You are reborn every day of your life and every day is a new day, every minute a new minute, and every moment is a new opportunity to fall in love with life.

What is Creating the Moments of Our Life?

If you look around and you're not in the right place, if the situation is all wrong or the people you are with are all wrong or you are married to the wrong person, and you accept the responsibility for the situation as your own creation, then you can begin to do something about it. But if you think it is due to that person or it is due to the situation or if only you had a bit of luck, things would be different, or if you hadn't been born this way or born into this particular family, it never works. You've got to look at every situation as *self-created*. The responsibility is yours for the life you're living and the consciousness you have and the reactions of other people that are brought to you through the actions or inactions of your own consciousness. Once you accept the responsibility, you know that you can do something about your situation. But as long as you're pushing it off and saying, "That's not me! I didn't create that. They created the situation. They're the problem, not me! The situation is the problem, not me!", you are helpless. You can never be master of yourself as long as you think your destiny depends on others.

You *are* the situation. Your consciousness has created your presence in that problem, whatever it is. The very first step is to accept responsibility for every pain, every thought, every problem that you have to deal with, instead of running away from it or saying, "It just happens that way." You can't become free or be able to leave behind those things that are binding and enslaving you if you don't first accept the responsibility for those things. Move *toward* the area of pain, the thing that is giving you the problem, rather than sweeping it under the carpet or running away or indulging in something else. Remain with it and grapple with it so that eventually it will melt away. Once you get mastery over it, there is no problem.

Many of the problems we have are solvable simply by greater resources. If it is a situation where we're in a bind because of money, or we have dependents, or we have a family—people who are looking to us as a source—maybe the whole problem can just be solved with an extra couple of thousand dollars, but if we're too proud to sell or to go out and make the $2,000 because of some idea we have about ourselves, then we're stuck. That dirty job we recoil from is the same thing as recoiling from a menial job because we're going to get our hands dirty and we'd rather pay somebody to do it rather than do it ourselves. We recoil from the problem, rather than going towards it and dealing with it and getting it out of the way. It may be that the only thing holding us up is that one little area where we don't want to go and do something, where we're not selfless enough to go and do the one thing that we hate most.

If you hate doing something, you're negatively attached to it. Hate and love are the same energy, just reversed. If you hate someone, your consciousness is always on that someone, always saying, "How can I get even with him?" You're always talking about your enemy. If you have a negative attachment toward things you don't like to do, the way to cut through and get flowing with the energy so that it pulls you along is to always do the things you don't like to do. If you go on and do them, very soon those things have no power over you. Even just being *prepared* to do them sometimes means you don't ever have to do them. Something in the cosmos knows your heart, and if you're prepared to go and do the dirty jobs, somehow it never gives you those jobs to do. It gives you some other jobs to work on.

It is very strange how this whole universe around us is like a total environment. It supplies everything we need for our growth; just like you put a seed in the ground and it germinates and has everything it needs to grow hidden within it, so in the same way, the universe around us has everything that we need at hand. We don't need any fancy places. We don't need any special Mercedes-Benzes or airplanes or fancy cooking stoves. There are people who can afford all that who live in a hovel. They could rent a fancy palace, but when you go to their room it is in a shambles. And they love that. They don't want to be in a fancy palace because it's a hassle. But those who want everything nice, nice buildings, nice lawns, nice motor cars sitting in the driveway, all those things, often their inner life is in a big mess, because to get those nice things, they're ignoring something else that's going on inside themselves.

If you concentrate on the mess, the rest is easy. The only thing that is blocking you is the things you never want to do or to face, the things you sweep under the carpet, the things you avoid. When you meet those challenges head on, you find they just disappear. They're not real problems. They're made of your consciousness and that's all. They're ghosts, will-o'-the-wisps.

We've been given the power to crush those problems and cut through them with our consciousness. And we can do it. But we can only do it if we have the *will*, and will means we put our heart into it. If we haven't got our heart into it and we're pussyfooting around the problem, not wanting to get into it properly and really deal with it, somehow it gets worse. It becomes an icky kind of spider web that closes all around you and you're just swallowed up in it all.

But if you approach the mess with the conscious thought, "I'm going to cut through. I'm going to master it. I'm going to get my consciousness out and wrap it around the problem and really sort this thing out, jump it up and down and deal with it," sometimes the problem is gone before you even get to it. Because you're sending out that vibration and the universe says, "Well, it's no use giving him this kind of problem, he's going to deal with it. He's dealt with it already in himself, so he doesn't need the problem. Let's give him something else."

The word "responsibility" comes from "response," the ability to respond. That is the key. Respond to the situation as something of your own making and don't indulge in the pleasure of doing only what you like. Do the things you don't like first, and then everything that is left is what you like.

Your Consciousness Works Miracles

I think the first thing that a person has to do in order to persist is to be convinced that it is worthwhile. That means developing some certainty that what you are doing is going to come off, sometime. If you don't have that certainty, then you will have uncertainty, and if you've got the slightest uncertainty about whatever you are doing, if you've got that certain little thing niggling in the back of your mind that maybe it's not going to work, then you bring about a state of darkness.

The doubt doesn't understand who the doubter is. There is no separation between the doubt and the doubter. The one who doubts puts the doubt there, and if you are not aware that you put the doubt there to destroy your feeling of certainty and sense of conviction about what you are doing, then you will keep on living in that uncertainty, not realizing that you yourself are creating it. The doubt and the doubter are one because we permit doubt rather than certainty. You will only achieve your goal when there is a sense of conviction. I don't like the word "faith," because so many people say they have it. But there is a saying that "he who has faith and has not love, his faith isn't worth anything." In other words, someone who has faith and has no works to show for it, his faith is just a bunch of hot air. He has not really got the conviction that his faith works, because if he did, then he would be putting it to work.

What nourishes a person is that feeling of certainty within, and that brings about a feeling of love, which is its own reward. Haven't you noticed how lovers quarrel when they begin to doubt each other's love? And what lovelight do you see in their eyes when love is certain! When you are that certain about your own love, you can love it and still leave it, for the truth of your love has succeeded.

And that is true for anything you think about—true for your life and what you're doing at this moment. Nobody will believe in you as much as you. If you don't believe in you, no one else will either. If something is not happening for you, there is only one person who can make it happen. That is you.

When you are absolutely certain in yourself, your consciousness begins to work for you in a totally different way than when you're hamstrung by doubts, resistances, pressures, all the things that turn you off. If you have an inner certitude, a sense of conviction, then your consciousness works miracles. It is the most potent stuff there is. It is the stuff that everything is made of and, ultimately, it is going to come out supreme. This is why Christ says temples and all those things will pass away "but my word will live on forever." He is talking from that state of consciousness.

THE GREAT SECRET

You can't do anything without a will to do it. If your will is not in it, if your heart is not in it, you can't win a game. If your heart is not in the game of chess, your head can't win the game. It doesn't matter what game you're playing—the game of life, the game of golf, the game of business, the game of love—any kind of game. If your heart is not in it, you can't win. Your success depends on you knowing this.

The simple clue is to ask yourself, when you sit down to play a game or do some work, "Is my heart in this? Do I really want to be here?" Your own inner voice will tell you clearly whether you'd prefer to be somewhere else. If there is somewhere else you'd prefer to be, then you should be integral with yourself and take your body there. If you're sitting somewhere where your heart isn't, you're wasting your time and making yourself miserable, because you're in conflict. It doesn't matter what the conflict is; if you're working inside the house and the sun is shining outside, and your heart is outside in the sun and here you are stuck inside the house, you have a problem. Your head says, "I've got to get this work done." Your heart says, "I want to be in the sun!" So you're torn in pieces because there is a war going on between your head and your heart. That is true in everything you do.

Will is the most powerful part of us. If there is no will to seek unity or harmony in life, there will not be any harmony. If there is no will to communicate in depth, at the level of the heart, there cannot be any true relationship, just surface relationship. If there is no will, there is no satisfaction, no fulfillment, no feeling of being "filled full."

If you want that filled full feeling, where you want to give because you're filled and overflowing, you have to be willing to go into the heart. That means you also have to be willing to be vulnerable. Without opening your heart, without making yourself vulnerable, how can you penetrate that space? It is not possible to be in the heart and also protecting yourself with a thick wall of fears and doubts and suspicions about life or about others. If we sit behind a thick wall in a castle, protecting ourselves from being hurt or being thought wrong, we can't get in the heart. We can only peer as through narrow slits at life from the battlements of that castle.

One of the clues to being in the heart—the simplest clue—is this: can you open yourself to be hurt? Is there any place in your heart where you can be hurt? And can you open yourself? Can you communicate with another person in such a manner that it doesn't matter what they say or what they do? If you're totally open in the heart, there is no way you can be hurt, because the heart is the totality of being. And a heart which has no bounds is a huge being indeed. So there is nowhere for the hurt to stick. There is nothing there to be hurt, because if you give love from that space, without calculating or without expecting any love in return, then you have become love, and all you are is love. All you radiate is love, and there is an inexhaustible supply. If people don't receive your love, it doesn't matter, you've got plenty more to give. If you keep radiating love when people try to injure you, you don't have to have a point where you can be wounded. If your heart is willing to keep on, you needn't be affected. If you're in the heart, no one can disturb you. It's only if you're in the head, in the ego, in the mind, that you *mind* things. Another simple clue is: do you mind? You say, "Do I mind what this person is doing?" If you are minding, then you're not in the heart.

Now it may be necessary, if you are in the heart, sometimes to be ruthless. You can seek harmony and unity and cooperation and you can give love endlessly to someone, and they will just take it, dash it to the ground and tread on it, turn it against you. By loving them, you are giving them the energy to hurt you if they can. So why pour endless love down the drain and waste it? Don't do that. Keep radiating love, but put it where it's going to be fruitful.

You see, in a way, there may be times when you have to be ruthless with yourself. Because the heart is your pure being. That is the place in you that is your real self. And so, in order to live with yourself, you may have to do things that your mind doesn't want to do. You may have to go against reason, go against what you like to do, in order to stay centered in that space where you cannot be separated from truth, because you can't be happy in your heart unless you're living in truth. And if you compromise with truth, you can't be in your heart. If you know there is something you're doing that is not right or if you are willing to compromise yourself, in business, in a relationship, or in anything, then it's not going to sit very easy in your heart. There'll always be a feeling that there is something missing, that the truth is not with you, and you'll be looking for it— always hunting, searching, looking for the truth "out there," instead of realizing it in here, in your heart.

So that is another simple clue: are you living in truth? Now, to the mind, it may seem hard to live in truth. The mind always thinks it is difficult to live truthfully. The mind says, "If I tell the truth, what will they think? If I speak the truth, I'll make some enemies. If I tell that person what I'm really thinking, my God!" The mind is not always living in the truth, and that is another way you tell whether you're in your heart, namely: is your mind arguing with the rightness of your actions or your thoughts? You can't be at peace or in harmony as long as there is some thought there that is making you uneasy with the truth. It is better you make life difficult by living in the truth, because in the end it's easier to live the truth than it is not to live the truth. The mind thinks, "If I live the truth it's going to be a real hard trip," but it isn't. It's simpler in the end and there are fewer problems to deal with.

If you don't go for the truth and stay prepared to sacrifice everything for it, you're always going to be uncertain and insecure. Whatever is in the heart is what creates our feelings. Sometimes it is a lack of certainty, a lack of security. If a person is running after money and only money, something in his heart is insecure. He wants to grab everything, simply because he's not feeling very certain about himself. He feels he doesn't have enough, even if he has lots and lots of money. This hunger in the heart makes him go out to conquer the world or become famous, and people like this can't stop themselves because they don't know where their insecurity is coming from, because they're not in touch with their heart. They live in their heads, thinking they can reason it all out: "If I do that, and I do that and that, then I'll be happy." But it doesn't work out, because their very insecurity in the heart—the feeling of lack—somehow makes them come on from the head, and so they don't have a proper relationship with the heart.

Those who are in their heart and express their true being become famous and lovable because they express themselves with truth. We call these people saints, but really there are more unfamous saints than famous ones. It's easy to know a well-known saint with a pedigree. But only a saint in the heart can recognize another saint standing right beside him or walking along a street. In the heart is where the real relationships are made—whether in business, in spiritual life, or friendships. They're all made from that vibration, a feeling of wanting to do something for that person without reward, not thinking, "What do I get out of it?" That sort of thing comes from the head, and relationships made at that level never succeed in giving security or the feeling of being "filled full."

The clue is always if you feel insecure and you're always running after or grabbing something or you're greedy for something, you look inside your heart and see where that insecurity is—what is it that you don't have or that's making you uncertain about yourself? So you look inside the heart and ask yourself: "Why is it that I'm chasing this or that? Why can't I sit still and just be at peace with myself?" These simple little clues that are manifesting around you in your relationships with others, in your relationships with the totality, amount to one total thing. Your being is where you act out your life. You cannot be anything other than your real heart. You can try to be something else with your head, but actually everything you do will be according to your will and the will is what your heart wants to do. So whatever you do will be conditioned by the heart. And that is the great secret—knowing that everyone is acting out of their true being, whether they like it or not. They cannot be anything or do anything other than what they really are in the heart. This law applies to the crook as much as to the saint. The only difference is that the saint knows the law and lives it. This is called surrender to the great secret.

THE SOURCE OF POWER

You can say a person is very willful, especially a child. Children know what they want to do and by gosh, they're going to do it unless you restrain them or win them around. So the will is really not in the head at all; it's not a question of your head dominating your heart. Your will is really in your heart. As a man *is* in his heart, so will be his will. Whether it is an individual or a group of people, if their heart is going one way and their head is going another, then there is a big conflict. Resistance develops and it becomes very hard to practice discipline. The word "discipline" is the origin of the word "disciple;" "disciple" means accepting a discipline. Discipline can be imposed from outside or imposed from within. To develop *will*, you first have to become a disciple, whether it is of a person who lived a long time ago, like Buddha or Christ, or whether it is of someone who is interpreting Buddha or Christ, or whether it is of someone with an original philosophy. We are still required to examine the contents of our consciousness, as this special person or those words or that philosophy is contrasted with the quality of our own life.

When we become a disciple, do we mean we have to force ourselves into a straitjacket and say, "Thou shalt not be or thou shalt be a certain way?" That is the kind of self-discipline where your heart is going in one direction and your head is going in another. Your heart wants to run around and play and your head says, "Nope, discipline." Your head becomes a no-no and your heart wants to be free. So your will is completely shattered in a way because there is no power in it.

The mind of human beings is very unruly and the emotions more unruly, so how do you get to that point where your discipline is easier. One of the ways of developing self-discipline is either to make your own ritual or join one that is already going. It's harder to make your own. Ritual itself originated from this difficulty of the human mind to be able to do a task spontaneously. By developing a method, a way of going about doing whatever you're doing, you can succeed. If you put it in the form of a ritual, it becomes easier because then you go on automatic. It's like driving a car. You don't have to learn to drive the car every day; you go through a little ritual. You switch the key on and you press the starter button, and you warm it up, and then you drive off. You don't think about this ritual once you've done it a few times.

It's no use trying to force your head into becoming a disciple. It will always be arguing inside yourself and making judgments all the way along the line about whether you should do what your teacher or your minister or your model says or what the book says.

You're rationalizing whatever you're doing, with your head. You are arguing with yourself. Whereas if your heart is there, your *will* comes very easily and powerfully, enabling you to accomplish the discipline without a lot of effort. In fact, you begin to enjoy it. If your heart is in something, it's like a hobby, something you *like* to do. If your heart is not in it, then you won't get any benefit; it won't work for you. There's no method in the whole earth, no technique in the whole earth that will work if you don't use it right, if you don't put your heart in it, because your heart and your consciousness are one. You can fiddle around in your head with some technique or other, but you'll never really get anything out of it, no enjoyment and not much results. It doesn't matter whether you're working a computer or are a carpenter with chisels and tools or whatever, if your heart is not in it, you'll never develop skill. It is the same with scientists. You'll never make that extra effort to improve yourself, your quality of action. To become a master is like playing a musical instrument. If you're just playing it because you feel you want to be great and your heart doesn't love the instrument or the sound, then your performance will be very ordinary and sterile. But if your heart is in it, you'll go a thousand miles just to get a lesson on how to improve just a little bit. You'll put in the time practicing. And in time, you will become expert at it. If you're really feeling the effects of self-discipline, whether you appoint someone else to discipline you like a teacher or whether you of your own free will decide to become a disciple and take a certain teaching or whatever, it will make no difference. Whenever you get benefit from your discipline, then it becomes pleasurable because you experience the growth. When you feel yourself growing and learning and loving it in spite of the effort and the difficulty, you know you can persist to the end. You know your effort is not in vain. You know that the pain is worth the result. There is no other reason a mother goes through the intense pain of labor and childbirth. Five minutes after she sees the results, she has forgotten the pain. Self-mastery and success are like that.

THE DEEPER MEANING
OF GOALS

There is a big difference between a *goal* and an *aim*. Aims may be realizable. Goals may never be realizable. You may set yourself a goal that is so far ahead of you that the more impossible the goal, the more you might advance as a human being. The higher you aim towards a goal that others think is impossible, the more you advance. If you even get halfway or maybe a third of the way, that might be a better way towards becoming a fulfilled human being. But these are goals and achievements which require help from others or help which comes from on high.

On the other hand, aims are something you can achieve with the capacities which you have been given. Obviously, if you have been given a very weak body with brittle bones, it is no use trying to carry flour sacks or cement; it is no use trying to fit yourself into a job for which you do not have the capacity. And similarly, a big strong man with lots of brute strength who is quite at home carrying flour sacks and has more brawn than brain, wouldn't want to be given jobs in mathematics or something that requires a lot of ingenuity and mental tenacity. Obviously, we must set our aims in terms of our gifts, our weaknesses, and our strengths, and not overestimate our capacity. Otherwise, when we do not achieve these aims we have set for ourselves, we will be disappointed. We may even consider ourself a failure because we set expectations we could not meet.

If we live an aimless life, one that doesn't seem to be getting anywhere or going anywhere, we might feel a lack of something. And yet, in the highest sense, is there anywhere to go? If we set self-knowledge as our highest goal, then where is there to go or to aim at? After all, the journey is from yourself to yourself and what shorter journey is there than that? And yet in another sense, that is the longest journey, because you must go around the whole universe just to come up behind yourself, as it were, sneak up behind yourself and look at your own consciousness.

If we have that self-knowledge as our goal, then that is an awfully long journey, for to get there, to sit in the seat of consciousness in a state of sublime peace, has only ever been achieved by a handful of people on the planet. Can we make this a goal? Can we succeed in terms of going straight to that place inside ourselves? It might be easier to do it in thought than to do it in fact. It might be easier to think that we are there sitting, as it were, very close inside ourself, knowing ourself very well, when in fact we might not know ourselves at all. We might not know where our limits are, where they begin and where they end. We may never even know if there is an end or a beginning to us, or what the means are by which we can get to that end, or even if there is any real separation between the means and the end. People tend to think in terms of techniques as means and then the technology itself becomes the end. Some examples are the space program, the atomic bomb, the telecommunications system. Does more technical communication, faster communication, television communication really improve what is said between humans? Of course not. We say no more important things over the telephone, the television or from the surface of the moon than were said in the time of the great Chinese philosophers or in the Psalms of King David one thousand years before Christ. It is very important to know this.

In the formulation of a goal, then, we have to be super careful not to think in terms of, "If we do this technique, we will get to that end." We can't set any goal without first realizing that whatever we bring to that experience is going to be made exactly of what we are.* In our thoughts and feelings we must realize always that we cannot be anything other than what we are. Whatever means we use to get to an end, there is always the problem of the user, the one who

---

*Christ expressed this thought written by the prophets 1500 years before him in the saying, "As a man thinketh so in his heart is he."

employs the means. However good the means may be, however smart the technique may be, the user of the technique is going to encounter himself or herself in the use of those means. We cannot be any better or more skillful than we are in our heart, in the center of our being, or any more dedicated to the goal than our consciousness is capable of being. And if we don't have control over our consciousness, how can we control the means by which we reach the end?

In setting ourselves a goal, we have to do so with the understanding that this is just an artifice, just something that we put in our consciousness like we put a peg on the wall to hang our hat on. We put a peg in our consciousness to hang ourselves on, because without that, what is there? What is there except an idea that we are a self? What is "I"? "I" is just a peg on the wall of consciousness on which you hang your ego, your self-sense, your idea that you are something. But is that something real? Is the ego real? Is the mind real? Is the self-sense real? Or is it just some fantastic delusion that we play on ourselves, like some cosmic game?

We like to trick ourselves, to deceive ourselves that there really is something separate from us out there, that there really is somewhere to go, like to the movies or falling in love, or even getting enlightened.

The list of cosmic shows is endless. It is only by identification with ourselves as a body that we create an inside and an outside. We ourselves create the somewhere to go. If we had no body and our mind was just a thought, it could go anywhere and be anything, could travel anywhere in the universe with the speed of thought. If we could be wherever we wanted to be in a flash of consciousness, where is there to go but where we are now? As fast as that, is an eternal moment in which our consciousness can travel from ourself to ourself.

Contrasting such an eternal moment with the nitty gritty work we must do on ourself to reach our individual aim or goal in life is what the spiritual life is all about. Why, if there is nowhere to go, do we have to work so hard to get to the Kingdom of Heaven? Why, if we are already there, do we have to travel all around the universe to find self-knowledge? When Christ spoke of the Kingdom of Heaven, he meant the unitive consciousness that knows no separation, no inside or outside. If we get sidetracked into being seen as an important person or being loved or respected or anything that must be won from outside us, from other people, then the natural unfolding of ourselves from the seed that is within us will not take place. Christ came to tell us of eternity and the Kingdom of Heaven which is just almost within our grasp. Yet he knew the goal of heaven on earth was only a theory, a promise or a vision until people could perfect their thoughts and actions. This was why he had great patience with mistakes and human errors born out of ignorance but was fiercely *im*patient with the self-righteousness and pride of those who would glibly condemn others but could accept no word of criticism themselves, or those who confused their aims and goals with their means of achieving them. By working on our motives, our emotions, our reactions, our attitudes and thoughts, we weed our garden. Then the seed of our uniqueness can grow and come to its flowering.

FEAR OF CRITICISM

How can we learn to be less touchy? Why is it that if you identify with your work, you have to do it perfectly because if you don't you won't feel that you're anybody, and when somebody criticizes even the slightest flaw in it, you take it personally? The first thing to realize is that work or sport or even play or art is a compensation. Any overidentification with work or play or some kind of skill or whatever it is you think is "you," means that when people criticize your effort, you get feelings of insecurity. Or perhaps you don't take the feedback or you can't learn from them, simply because you are afraid to think that your work might not be good work. The only cure for that is really to be so totally open that you don't have to become defensive about your work. Whatever your work or skill is, you must show what your real feelings are to someone rather than blocking the feelings off and consequently secretly blocking off the person who is criticizing. Identifying with your work is a compensation for not being able to communicate openly by other means. If you resist the feedback from someone or throw up a wall, it could be because you were born that way. It could be that you came into this life with that problem, that particular thing to work on. While other people have other problems, maybe your problem is to learn to open up and not be afraid of being criticized or having your work inspected by another so that you become very defensive at the slightest comment made about it, taking it all personally.

You usually find that people who have that problem from birth have a particular facial expression. It's called a "stiff upper lip." And people with this problem do have a stiff upper lip. Whenever you're talking to them, trying to get through, their lip comes down solid, and it's always twice the length of anybody else's. Measure the distance between the nose and the lips and you'll see that people with the very long lips never take feedback, never listen. Leonid Brezhnev was a perfect Party Chairman because he never listened to anybody. People who are super-open to the slightest criticism, on the other hand, have very short lips. The long-lipped people erect a wall. Everything is always stopped by that wall, so that they can't be criticized. Short-lipped people take everything very sensitively and are hurt easily by what people say.

If you realize that you have a stiff upper lip, look in the mirror and watch your lips. Realize that when people are talking with you, you are making your lip rigid and saying, "I'm not listening, my mind is made up, my mind is closed; others listen, not me."

You can begin to work on this problem by doing the opposite when someone is criticizing you. Tell yourself, "I can learn from this. I don't have to shut it out; I don't have to be afraid of it. My image of myself is not going to be injured if I let it in and open myself to it." Anything that is rigid, like a really hard shutter that is rigid with iron bars on it, will cause people to have to use a sledgehammer to get anywhere. They say something and you don't hear, so they say something a little stronger and you still don't hear, so they say something a little stronger still and you still don't hear, and every time they get more intense, your shutter goes up higher. So you still don't hear, and then they have to crash down on you. Some people are like that.

You can avoid having that explosion happen. If you realize that your identification with whatever you're doing is your compensation for not opening yourself up and expressing yourself, then you can begin to work on not taking criticism personally but welcoming it, so that you can improve your work. It's like a musician who wants to learn. If you're just a small-time musician, of course, you don't like people talking bad about your playing, but if you're a top one, a concert pianist or someone very good, you'll always listen to your competitors, because you want to learn a trick or two to make you even better. Those people will even pay a fee for criticism. Imagine a top pianist going to another concert pianist who's just slightly better, and saying, "Give me a lesson." And he says, "Okay, I'll charge you a thousand dollars." And the other says, "Well, it's worth it, just to learn one thing more." That's how they are. I know a few of them. They will go to the best in the world and pay any fee just to get that little much better. Compare that to most people, who bristle at the slightest comparison with others.

That seeking the best, of course, is seeking perfection, it is seeking to be the ultimate. Not everyone bothers, because not everyone wants it that bad. But if you can always adopt that attitude that you're searching for criticism, searching for some way to improve your work, then you become open and you seek people's advice, you seek their help, and you seek different ways of doing things. Then you do become a star performer and people can relate to you. But if you are rigid and you think you're a star performer and you identify with all that and yet in fact you're not, then people will always put you down. They're always trying to get at you somehow and when they can't get to you, they have to get heavier and heavier and heavier with their battering at the doors. You don't realize that when you get spoken to in a heavy manner that it's often your own fault. People have to speak louder and louder and louder until they're practically screaming just to get you to hear. You don't realize that you are causing that because if you were sensitive to the other person at all, then just a whisper would be able to get through.

The problem is really the rigidity in our ego structure, our self-image, that shuts out any thought because we're a bit afraid that we might not be who we think we are or who we want to be. We might not be as good, might not be as perfect, might not be as skillful, and we can't tolerate that thought somehow. So we compensate for it by shutting out truth. To become more open, we have to learn to seek criticism or feedback and be able to take it.

DEVELOPING CONFIDENCE

To develop self-worth, you have to have some accurate knowledge about yourself or about whatever you are doing, so that when you respond to people, you respond from some self-confidence in yourself. Self-worth really means self-confidence, not overconfidence, which means an overestimate of yourself. It means knowing what you're talking about or shut up, knowing when to say you don't know and a willingness to go out to get the knowledge to do the job. If you rely on just happening to stumble upon knowledge that you need to do a particular work, you'll always get caught in some degree of blindness because you're not aware of what you don't know.

It is important to acquire *certain* knowledge. By "certain" I mean living in certainty by testing everything, not assuming or making assumptions. Whenever there is a doubt, you ask yourself, "Do I really know this?" or "Do I know what to say if a customer called me and asked me this question?" If you have to answer, "No, I wouldn't be able to," then the thing to do, even if it's the middle of the night, is get up and get that book or telephone somebody or do something so that you are no longer in doubt. If you're in doubt, you're uncertain and you're going to be working in fear that you're going to trip or make a mistake. As long as you have that fear, you won't have confidence. And when you don't have confidence, your relationships with others will suffer because they will feel your weakness and they will not only trade on it but they'll waste your time. If you don't answer their questions precisely, because you lack the knowledge, they won't give you any respect. If you don't have respect, you won't be able to run a business.

It's like a very intricate web; all these things are connected and they all come back to certain kinds of knowing. You can know by intuition if you've got that gift. Some people can do things just off the top of their head, because they are born with it or they have developed that skill. Often they're fooling people, of course; they walk out in front with a banner and say, "Look, follow me, I know the way," when really they don't; they're just hoping to be a step ahead of the next guy. That's what we call a politician. They don't really know any more than anybody else but they pretend to, and so we all say, "Yeah, you govern us. You take the wheel. Steer our ship of state." If you have the gift of real intuition and know what's coming in the future, then you can rely on that, but you have to test that intuition and not just assume it is right and that you can get away with it every time.

There is another kind of knowledge, exact or mathematical knowledge, as in two plus two equals four, in which everything must be double-checked. That's precise knowledge. In this realm, you don't assume that you've got $16,000 in the bank when it might be $14,000, because if you write a check without doing your books and balancing your statement, you're going to make a big mistake some time, and it might be just the wrong time to make a big mistake.

There are other kinds of knowledge too, of course, besides mathematical knowledge. There are inference and induction, which are rather philosophical. Basically, you don't have to test everything if you've done it already 50 times. It is reasonable to presume that the sun will rise tomorrow morning, even though it is not absolutely certain, because the universe could blow up between now and then. The universe is full of such hazards and we have to live with them. The possibility that the sun might not rise is a rather remote one from our point of view, so that kind of inference is all right. But there are many that we live by that aren't all right, because the chances are much smaller that they'll happen. We run our lives and leave many more chances open by relying on other people or pushing responsibility off when we should take it ourselves. Thinking someone else will do something when you're not sure they will is where people fail. By just making that extra effort or caring a little more about your performance and skill, you can avoid those pitfalls and you gradually get a feeling of confidence that you can do things. But not if you're always half-baked and unsure. If people ask you questions and you don't really know the answer, you come across weak.

What you have to do is go and get the knowledge, even if it's in a narrow area. Be strong in that area so that if anybody asks you a question, you're the authority; you're the one who knows every inch of the floor. In that way, you will feel more secure and make fewer mistakes. You don't have to know *everything*. You just know to the extent of your capacity and do your best. But if your best is defeated by not going out to get the skill, not going out to get the certain knowledge and just trusting to luck or to providence, you're not really being master of yourself because your destiny then depends on so many other factors, so many other people, so many other circumstances that are out of your control. The way to get control of yourself, your own consciousness, is to know your own weaknesses. To know yourself is the highest knowledge. You must always know precisely and exactly where your weakness is so that you can make an extra effort in that area. Because you may get by on your strong points, but it's the weak points that are going to bite you in the heel.

Working on our weaknesses also improves our strengths because in the end we will have less work to do. But working on our weakness is not pleasant work and usually it means doing something we just don't want to do. Selfish people hate working for the benefit of others, and it doesn't come naturally at all. Spiritual people hate working in the business world and the contentious world of law and money. If we are to improve the world we must do the tasks that no one else wants to do and face the problems that everyone wants to sweep under the carpet.

We must go towards the unpleasant, not run away from it. We must face the painful situation, not avoid it. We must deal with every huge problem while it is still small. All big problems start small like weeds in the garden. If we are lazy and don't pull them up, a thousand seeds will sow themselves. By taking action now, before our weaknesses come home to cancel out our strengths, we can become victorious over our own ignorance of self. When doing what you don't like becomes easy, you are master of yourself and gain a sense of conviction about who you are.

OVERCOMING A NEGATIVE SELF-IMAGE

Most human beings at some time or another have doubts about themselves, doubts about whether they really are as powerful or as attractive as others are. And of course they tend to give themselves bad publicity by always talking about their failures. It often seems that they are attached to their negative self-image as much as some people are attached to their positive images. Other people are always selling themselves as Number 1 and giving the impression they are really tops and walking around puffed up with pride, or they are always patting themselves on the back. And you often find that such people are out of balance; they have a high self-image but they don't *perform* that way. If you were to judge on their performance alone, it would not be very high. But inside, they've got to have a puffed-up image to compensate for their feelings of inferiority. The negative self-image is just the other, inflated side of that same coin. And if you've got a whole group of people with negative self-images, then they re-inforce each other. They tend to sit around in a very low energy state trying to create some intensity or excitement, because excitement isn't really going on inside them. If they were really bubbling with life and feeling excited, they wouldn't have a negative self-image.

But when you feel empty and kind of down and you don't know what to do next with your life, and your self-discipline is slipping and you don't really seem to be getting on or going anywhere, you're taking two steps forward and three back, then you tend to talk about your failures. It's like some people talk about every detail of their operations, what the doctor said, what the doctor did. Some people tell you their life story like that. You have to sit there and listen to all the gory details, the negative stuff, bit by bit, never missing out on even one little shred. And it's boring.

What it amounts to is that they are obsessed with themselves. People only get a negative self-image when they're really obsessed with themselves. It's a kind of social disease in a way, to be so wrapped up in your own thoughts that you can't give of yourself or radiate. Because if you radiated—and I don't mean just putting on an act, because people see through that, I mean radiating without saying a word—people simply feel good in your presence and they respond to you. But if you *try*, it will come across stilted and artificial. People can sense that and they'll be suspicious, so if they respond to it at all, it will come back funny. You don't have a negative self-image when you feel that people respond to you positively. But if you're not getting positive feedback from outside and people are not mirroring back to you some warmth, then you tend to put yourself down into a low-energy state. That's the difference between low-energy people and high-energy people. High-energy people are not obsessed with themselves. They can risk getting their image a little tarnished. They can risk their ego. They're not feeling that kind of inferior feeling that believes if they did what they really wanted to do and said what they really wanted to say, that they'd be put down or misunderstood or not thought well of.

People who can risk all that are not obsessed with themselves or their self-image and so they don't need to compensate. Compensation for a negative self-image usually means putting on some self-importance or getting drunk or indulging in all kinds of hedonism. It's a compensation for feeling like a dull person, craving stimulation or excitement in your life and always looking for it outside yourself. You go like a butterfly from one thing to the next. But the only real way is to get stimulated from within. And then your negative self-image is blown away. Just like when you come into a dark room and switch on the light, the darkness disappears completely. You have to start pumping out some energy, and you can't do that when you are obsessed, because the energy is looping; it's short circuiting around and around inside you and never gets outside your skin, so people don't feel any warmth radiating from you. There is plenty of energy churning inside, but it's all contained within this one vessel.

When people don't feel any warmth communicated from you, they don't give you any warmth back and somehow it is hard for them to bridge the gap. It seems a bit phoney to make any advance towards such a person because there is nothing coming from them. It's all locked up in an obsession. If we keep worrying about it in our own minds and keep feeding the obsession, then we never will solve the problem. We have to be able to risk not being so concerned with Number 1, not taking ourself so seriously. Follow the eleventh commandment, "Thou shalt not take thyself too seriously." Then it doesn't matter if your image gets tarnished. You'll find that you can relate to others more easily, and when you relate to them with ease, their warmth and energy will come flooding back to you in great abundance.

Look for the Light

You have a choice to go toward the dark or toward the light. If you turn toward the self-conscious, the self-obsessed, then your life will be full of compulsions, because there will be unknown phantoms and shadows in your consciousness that will pull you this way and that way. Fears will rise in your mind because you won't understand your mind. Your mind won't be full of light; it will be full of dark corridors and caves where the ghosts lurk waiting to jump out to get you. You'll either be very paranoid or you'll be always self-obsessed with your feeling of weakness, your lack of confidence and insecurity about life. You won't trust anyone. You won't trust life. If you choose the selfish dark force, the power, the fame, money or other gods, then your guide becomes your ego and the ego never feels good with itself. The ego always relies on its own power because egocentric obsession has cut itself off from the whole and has become a small part. It is always seeking confirmation from outside. Light force always springs up as confidence from within, whereas the dark force brings distrust. The egocentric self-image motivates you with fears and suspicions, and propels you to doubt yourself. So you will be always beset by selfish forces pulling at you, like a lot of demons, pulling you this way and that, trying to get you to create a better self-image of yourself. But why do you need a better self-image of yourself? Why do you have to do compulsive acts to get a better self-image? Because the self-regarding sentiment of our ego sense is attached to all that darkness, all that weakness, all those doubting ghosts. Our mind and body are like a temple which can be filled with angelic thoughts. But many people choose to fill the temple full of dark suspicion. One ray of light would disperse the whole lot. It sweeps the temple clean of darkness. You come into a dark room, you throw the light switch, and what happens? Darkness instantly disappears.

All compulsion, all fears, all those demons and pulls and desires drag us away from the light, because we only have the *thought* of light. To dynamically *live* a life of light means we have to identify with light every second. To switch on the light we have to *see* light, look for light, just like some people are always looking for sex. If they looked for light like they look for sex, they wouldn't have any problems, because if you look for light first, sexual fulfillment will come automatically. Put sex first and you'll always have compulsions; there will always be fears and insecurities, because as long as you put that first, you'll never really get enough of what you want, you'll never possess it. A person won't want to be possessed for that reason, and so it will always elude you, and as long as fulfilling sex is eluding you, you'll feel insecure. And as long as you feel insecure, you will have some fears about yourself. And as long as you have fear, there will be certain ghosts lurking round the corner, and you will have a very poor self-image even if you are rich and powerful. Those ghosts will always drag you down as they have brought down all the mighty, from the beginning of time.

Someone who is into light every second of the day doesn't have a poor self-image, because that person doesn't think of himself that much. Such people are not self-obsessed with power or fame. And that is a blessing, not having any self-image to worry about. If you're really into light, it'll just burn a poor self-image away. And you'll *feel* very light, because you don't have to live up to other people's expectations. You will not depend on their opinion of you. You won't have to compulsively act to create a good image in their minds of you. You just be yourself, and they can take it or leave it.

GREATNESS OF SPIRIT

Sometimes those who seem to have the most confidence actually don't have any real feeling of self-worth at all and are always living in fear of saying something that might ruffle someone else's feathers, especially the people that they work with or people who are in positions of authority. So inside themselves they feel they are quite lowly and humble, but others may see a big ego and say that they are arrogant or bossy. Why aren't people seeing on the outside what is going on in the inside? Perhaps it is because there is a great difference between genuine humility and self-denigration. The fear of disagreeing with people is really a fear of not being recognized or risking perhaps that someone will not like you or will not think highly of you. So what is it inside a person that wants to be thought highly of? The only fear there is, is ego fear. Certainly a humble person doesn't crave such recognition. So is it true humility to feel lowly or be always looking up to others?

I think that most of the greatest people have never had any doubt about where they are on the scale of evolution. But such a great person, who is perhaps at the top of the scale, has a true humility before God, or before that which is so far beyond anything human. That kind of humility is not always looking at itself and saying how guilty and wrong and sinful it is by comparison with other living things. It is not really comparing itself; it doesn't have any airs or assumptions or expectations about itself or craving for its needs to be recognized by others. A great person is only looking for recognition from his own highest self, not from others, and so he can risk his self-image. He can risk being thought wrong. He can risk being thought bad of. He can speak the truth and not worry whether that truth agrees with the truths of others.

You have to discriminate very carefully what the ego is doing, because in self-denigration there is an ego trip, in the sense that you are not standing up and saying, "I'm the greatest, look at me," but you're saying, "I'm so humble. I'm the lowest of the low." In a sense, that is putting yourself down so far that no one else can put you down any lower. It's a psychic defense mechanism. In that way, you create a mask, the ego creates a protection for itself. But the real desires are behind that mask, craving for the recognition of greatness. So what comes across is a person hiding behind a mask. True humility is not hiding behind a mask. It's getting in front of the mask and being willing to be exposed, willing to be laughed at, willing to risk what anyone says by speaking the truth that you believe in, even though people may disagree.

Hiding behind a mask is like being in a castle. When the enemy comes, you're behind those walls with a certain amount of protection, but you're also living in fear because you're all alone behind the battlements and all you've got is a narrow slit to look through. You can shoot your arrows just at a few people, because that's all you can see through that slit in the battlement. When you know there are thousands of people on the other side of that slit, it makes you feel afraid. The walls are thick and very comforting and give you a certain amount of protection, but looking through the slit at the universe does not give you an accurate picture of the total scene. So those people who are looking at you looking through the slit actually have a better view of you than you have of yourself.

You're sitting behind a mask, thinking certain thoughts, living in a certain amount of fear. But what is coming through to others is the reverse ego trip, the ego putting on an appearance of someone who knows that everything is okay, knows all the answers, doesn't want to take any advice from anyone, doesn't want to listen, always knows better. That psychological armor is the protection for the little person inside who is afraid. Why is he afraid? He's afraid he might lose the respect or recognition of others if he really gets out there in front of the battlements and exposes himself to all the arrows that might come.

Now it's not easy to come out from behind a mask. Nearly everyone is hiding something of themselves, not willing to risk all. Very few people are totally spontaneous in what they say or think because they're always thinking about reactions, about what is going to come back on them if they open their mouth too wide. It's a very human thing. But it is a fact that all humans who worry about that are unhappy. It's only when you can lose your fascination for your own self, for your own ego trip that you can let go of that fear. Self-esteem is a fine thing. You should respect yourself. But which self do you respect? If you respect the little self, the one that's craving to have attention from others, then this is going to be a problem. But if you respect your larger self, the greater self that isn't just in one little person but is in all other selves as well, you automatically get self-respect. The minute you begin to respect the beings of others and begin to think and feel from their inner worlds, whether you agree with them or not, that respect comes back to you. This doesn't mean you've got to be like them, but at least you have to first respect them enough to hear what they are like, before you disagree with them. If you tune in to a person and you think with them as they are speaking, you understand what they are saying; then you come on from your being, if it happens to be different, and you risk that they won't feel that you are a great enemy or a big boss or some kind of know-all. They will feel that they have been understood, even though you are different. So by respecting another's being, somehow you gain the self-respect which is a pure self-respect, not just something that you expect to get without performing something great. There is nothing wrong with feeling that you're great, but then you have to do great things, because if you feel you're great and you never do anything great, then you're kidding yourself.

Look at others, maybe even in your own family, maybe your own father thinks he's great but never does anything great. So you use your father as a model. The father always wants the son to do what he doesn't do himself. He wants the son to be great, to fill up all the gaps that he's got in his own being, so the son has got to toe the line, "Do everything right; all the things that I didn't do, you'd better do." That kind of thing. If you study your parent you get a mirror image of how you became like you are, and you can learn from it, because you see the mechanism so much clearer when you observe it in another. Then you don't have to worry about humility and putting yourself down and losing all your self-respect. It's a negative ego trip to waste your consciousness on such things. It's a sort of self-pity.

How do you get beyond the need for self-esteem? They teach self-esteem in classrooms now. I guess all the self-esteem is knocked out of people from the age of five or whatever, so they have to teach it in the classroom. But that's not going to give any real self-esteem. True self-esteem does not have to be shored up and reinforced from outside; it's something that springs from deep within, from respect for others. If you can respect others, you will automatically have self-respect. If you love others, you'll automatically love yourself. You can't love others without loving yourself. It's impossible. If you have no love in you, how can you love others? In word? In name? True love can't help loving others. And it's the same with respect. Self-recognition comes from recognizing the beings of others. Then the gap in communication disappears. If you respect the other person, then somehow, no matter what you may think of yourself, they respect you.

THE NEED FOR SELF-CONFIRMATION

Self-confirmation is usually pursued by building a reputation, becoming famous, being the great author, the great preacher, the great lawyer or doctor, the great scholar. We're brainwashed to succeed, to be strivers. We're brainwashed to go out there and elbow our way through society to get to the top, so we project this image of "success" even on our great spiritual leaders. We put them on the top of the pyramid, the top of some spiritual heights, and try to climb up there—to be number one, right alongside them. But that isn't how those people really are. They are constantly receiving confirmation not from down below, because most people don't understand the kind of consciousness that is at the pinnacle, but they receive from above. That kind of self-confirmation comes in a different way from the way we normally experience it.

Even a great man like Christ had to have confirmation from another. This isn't much like the Christian religion as it is taught, where Jesus is supposed to be sitting on the right hand of God. He's not supposed to need any self-confirmation, but he did seek it of John the Baptist. He wanted to be baptized by the Holy Spirit and, as you remember the story, John did recognize him coming down the path and said, "This is the one I've been speaking of." When Jesus asked him to confirm him, John refused. He said, "No, I can't confirm you, you have to confirm me," but Christ said, "No, you've got to do it. You have to baptize me, because otherwise I can't know that I really am who I think I am." So in that state of humility, he was baptised, and at that moment, confirmation came and he had a vision of the heavens opening up and a loud voice speaking to him inside his head saying, "I'm well pleased with thee."

So even at that supreme height of human endeavor, self-confirmation had to come. Now you can get it in social terms by striving to become famous, and ordinary people will worship you and put you on a pinnacle, but they won't make you happy. Most people who are famous are miserable because they've spent all their consciousness on getting famous so they never have much inner life of any worth. They sought the wrong things. So they marry two or three times—even six or ten times. The curse of fame is that having got everything that we can get on earth, there is still in us a spiritual search, a craving or desire that is in the heart of everyone.

So that deeper kind of confirmation comes from working on ourselves, working to receive that feeling from our higher self that we are okay. Can you get it from another human being? A man can get confirmation from a woman he loves, but it can only come when she totally trusts him enough to surrender to him. But will she ever surrender if she thinks that he's going to use her love or abuse her love or do other than glorify her love? So the easiest way to get that earthly kind of confirmation is to put all your attention on becoming eligible for some higher confirmation that doesn't come from people but comes from the cosmos around you, by making yourself eligible in your consciousness. Some people would say this is recognition from God but I believe that recognition from God can only come from within, from your own state of consciousness. Everything and everyone is already recognized by God, but not everyone has an understanding or recognition of who God is. We are told God is that, God is this, God is love, God is glory, etc., but can we tell *who* God is? Only life itself can tell who God is and when God is confirming us.

By purifying your consciousness, you're able to get confirmation from life all around you. There are little signals, little messages. You can tell when life is confirming you because all doors are opening. It doesn't mean you won't have a lot of difficulties, because once you enter a higher vibration, you'll find a lot of people trying to knock you down, because it's uncomfortable to them and shows them up. They feel threatened that you really don't need any confirmation from them or the system they believe in.

Now, self-confirmation, at every level of being, is available depending on where you put your consciousness. If you want confirmation as a famous person, you put all your consciousness on getting fame. If you want it from a woman, you put all your consciousness on serving that woman, and she will confirm it back. A woman really conquers a man by surrendering, and once she's totally surrendered to a man, he's hooked on that confirmation because he can't find that kind of surrender everywhere, so he will always come back to that one.

In the same way, for you to receive confirmation from the One, you have to surrender. It is a special surrender in that sense, because this is the way you receive cosmic recognition. You can understand that after you surrender, your will is not your own, it is the will of the cosmos, and in that influx of spirit you begin to radiate another kind of being that doesn't need to say, "I'm number one, I'm this or I'm that." Your being will be radiating what you really are and that will automatically bring you confirmation from others. You are "in the spirit" so to speak.

You don't have to be concerned with the confirmation itself; you have to concern yourself with being eligible. Put all your consciousness on becoming eligible for that influx of the spirit, and then, just like a light attracts moths, you'll have all the confirmation you can handle.

John the Baptist gave Christ the recognition even before he arrived, because he could see the vibration in the way he walked, in his eyes, in his aura. That's what we strive for, not for the cultural brainwash, but to be so centered that that vibration or radiation of being, speaks for itself. Then you don't have to say, "I'm number one. Look at me. Recognize me. Don't you know I'm very close to being a Jesus Christ or something?" Jesus Christ never was like that. People would say to him, "You're the one," and he'd say, "How do you know that?" He would see that as confirmation that the One was speaking through somebody, recognizing him, because he knew that only the One in a person can see the One in someone else.

Once you have that kind of confirmation, you feel secure. You just are what you are. You don't need to put out any fancy image. You just be yourself—your vulnerable self.

BECOMING A NEW PERSON

I don't know if you saw Yasser Arafat on the television recently when he said, "We're going to go on killing and fighting until the whole world changes its attitude." He was giving the world an ultimatum that he is going to keep bringing Beirut or whatever down around him in flames until the world changes. Not *him*. *He* does not have to change his method or his way of achieving his goal. Now, if we look back through our past relationships, maybe we too can see a pattern where we have demanded that other people change in order to have a relationship with us. And if they don't, then we give them an ultimatum and we break the relationship off. That is called being ruthless with others, just as Arafat is being completely ruthless with others. What he really needs to do is point the finger inwards and be ruthless with himself. All of us need to really see ourselves as we are—not as we think we are, or as we would like to be, or as we would hope to be, but how we actually are—and to be totally honest with ourselves and not try to whitewash our motives. If we arrive at our version of truth without doing this pointing of the finger inwards, we are most likely to have a very twisted and one-sided version of truth.

How do you change this? You watch your motives closely, by asking yourself, in anything you do, are you doing it for others or for yourself? Whether you do something good, bad or whatever, ask yourself the motive behind your doing it. And be honest. If you do something nice for someone, there could still be an ulterior motive for doing that. By asking yourself and being ruthless with yourself, you are able to come to some real change, not just on the surface but something that works deep within your own soul, because you will have that attitude which constantly questions your own integrity, your own quality. You examine the quality of your consciousness, the quality of your actions, the quality of your being, the quality of your giving, the quality of your seeing. Ask yourself if you are really capable of looking at the gaps in your consciousness. How is it possible to see those gaps if you don't know the gaps are there? You have to question yourself at every moment. Where are the gaps that I am not seeing? By ruthlessly exposing your own gaps rather than waiting for other people to give you ultimatums about your gaps, you gradually rise in the quality of your consciousness.

If you already think the quality of your consciousness is gapless, then you could be suffering from some form of pride that is due for a fall. If you are so full of self-pride that you believe you can say and do anything, get away with anything, wiggle your way around or through anything without consequences, you may be able to get away with it on the surface, but ultimately it's going to catch up with you. Isn't it easier to catch up with yourself first rather than waiting for others to point out those gaps? In that way you're able to advance in self-knowledge rapidly rather than slowly or not at all. If you refuse to look at your gaps or refuse to try and discover them or even acknowledge that there are some gaping holes, then you're going to remain at a standstill.

Anyone who reaches a comfort zone in the soul and feels that he does not have to move on or does not have to change or does not have to grow, is going to die spiritually, because life is growth, life is movement, life is action. As long as you are living, you're acting. If you're not acting, if you're not moving or remain standing still in your life, then eventually you'll have a spiritual death just like a tree that stops growing. It doesn't grow more cells or pull any more water up to the tips of its branches; it is dry and rigid. So the first wind that comes along snaps it. If there is life in it, it's springy, it's green, it's growing, it's living, and it can bend to the buffeting winds or to the forces that play on it; it can spring back. But if it becomes rigid, just as when a person becomes rigid in consciousness, unable and unwilling to change, then he too will be snapped by life.

Which is easier? The choice is yours: to be

part of the living, the changing, the growing or to be part of the dead, the rigid, the stale world that is not willing to grow? Unconsciously, human beings are either dead-seeking or life-seeking. In your unconscious mind, in your deepest being, you are either seeking something new, something green and living, or you are seeking to stay the same so that you won't have to change.

People who feel uncomfortable with change become very narrow, unwilling to listen, unwilling to respond to a changing world, and they try desperately to stop change from happening, because it becomes unbearable. About 99 percent of the world doesn't really want to change, and that is why it's so difficult to get anything new done. It's so difficult to have a New Age, a millenium. Just imagine if you had a new idea how people could live or what new food they might eat. Or supposing you were like Jesus with a new idea of God which differed from 2,000 years of mosaic law, would you really be willing to be crucified for it?

Every age says, "The New Age is coming," but it never does. Why not? Because the world is unwilling to make the change within that will permit a new world to be born. People think they are willing but they also think they can have the new world without changing themselves, and that is impossible. The only way the world will ever change is if *you* change. To have something new and different, you have to have that quality of consciousness that is willing to take responsibility for bringing the change about. And that cannot happen unless everyone can be open to do something new, not only externally but internally within themselves. Unless their consciousness is always new and they are willing to look for the new and willing to bring about the change that makes things new, they can't be part of that New Age. People who can't rethink their whole existence will always oppose anything untried. And even that which is tried and a great success will be a threat to those who cannot change their mode of thinking or their feeling about themselves. They'll bring the new idea down, rather than enhance it.

The secret of the new society or the secret of a new community is the secret of a new person—a person who is remaking himself, shaping himself, looking into the quality of his own life and cutting out what stops the change from happening. Unless you can cut through the blocks ruthlessly, you'll never be part of that new thing that is happening. That way sounds very absolute and foreboding to those people who are not yet convinced that this is a secret to happiness. But the fact is that I have tried making a new community of very well-wishing people at numerous locations and times, in order to prove it or disprove it. And after 25 years of actual experimentation with groups of willing people, I have come to the conclusion that those who cannot welcome change, who cannot love light enough to change old patterns in their lives and who cannot love the love light more than themselves, will never reach ultimate success and fulfillment. This is what Christ was saying to the rich young ruler and to Nicodemus. To the young prince he said give up the thing that you are most attached to, which in his case was his wealth and possessions; to Nicodemus he was saying you have to reshape your whole life, forget the past, forget your position, become "as a little child," be born again. Then you have the chance to do everything differently. This is a hard and sometimes frightening prospect, but there is no other way, no short cut, no parroting of the words "born again," while still clinging to the false belief that your way is the only way and that the job of total change can be done once and for all. We have to be born again daily if the words are to have any meaning and if the dogma is to be left behind.

Do It Now

It is natural for all human beings to be resistant to change, because that quality gives them a certain amount of stability. A schizophrenic has a mind that changes every second, even in mid-sentence. Distracting thoughts, distracting situations create instability, so the human mind has been made in such a way that it will resist change. It will automatically hang on to tried doctrines. How do you break through this natural immunity to life, which is always changing? How can you be green and grow, be supple and pliant? How can you release yourself from dogma, from fixed minds? This is not a rhetorical question but a matter of life and death spiritually speaking. Another factor is that too much change without control or power to assimilate that change is no good. If we go faster than we can take, if our development is pushed too far beyond our natural capacity, then we go bonkers. On the other hand, inability to change to the new, means to become rigid and stiff and deathlike. Slothfulness, the inability to lift yourself up from a situation, or the tendency to wallow in procrastination, is the second enemy of the spirit, next to self-righteousness. Slothfulness has many disguises and one of them is procrastination.

When you see someone making progress, often they are *using* the difficulties or resistances in themselves. When a challenge is offered, they take that challenge as an opportunity for lifting themselves up, whereas a procrastinator will put it off, saying, "Oh, I'll do it another time. I can't bother now." Really the very thing the procrastinator needs to do is to look at the consequences, namely, "If I do not deal with this small thing now, it will become a big thing later on."

Sometimes it's only a small thing holding us back, but it is a thing we don't want to face, so we push it under the carpet and pretend it's not there. We don't want to shake ourselves up and face the fact that we've go to do it sooner or later, so why not do it now. And of course, if we are holding back like that, we delay as long as it is possible, until the crisis comes and the ship is sinking. Some people need an awful lot of pain, an awful lot of negative thoughts and situations before they will actually make up their minds to change. When you finally go and do the thing, you find it was easy. You could have done it five years ago and been clear of it, without it bothering you and annoying you all the time.

People, being human, when they respond to life through that mechanism of rigidity, create stability and a feeling of security. They say, "It's threatening for me to have to change." But when you push away the challenge that life is offering you, then you're no longer using life as a means of growth. You hold back, hoping you won't have to do it. But there is no escape from the laws of consciousness, any more than there is escape from the laws of matter; they're just as immutable. There is no way out, even though the human mind is always looking for it. The ego is always looking to escape, always looking for the rat hole to run down. If there is any hole at all, it's going to find it, because the ego does not want to change. It does not want to give up its own feeling of self-worth. Because of that unwillingness to look at itself, it's always looking for a chink it can squeeze through to avoid being cornered.

People who are growing, who are not procrastinators, who "do it now" are the people who go towards the challenge and do not run away from it. When these people see a chink for the ego to wriggle out of, they block it up and say, "Now, that's not going to work. I'm going to have to come back and do that work, if I go through that chink; I'm going to have to do the work anyway, so I might as well do it now, because if I don't do it now, it will only be more difficult later on." These are the people who understand that every great task has to begin with a small beginning, a small step. The most difficult step of a long journey is the first one, particularly if you know it's going to be a long haul. And the easiest one is the last. Great things are done by doing small things in the beginning. If you can tackle a big problem while it is still small, it's easy.

Conversely, small problems always lead to big ones if you don't attend to them. They get worse and worse and more entrenched and our life feeds those problems until they become major obstacles. The longer we put off dealing with them, the tougher they become.

You only have to look at the world situation to see how every enormous issue begins small, whether it is an international incident or peace between nations or whatever. If you look at the origins, it always began as some little niggling thing that could have been dealt with on the spot. And the same in human relationships, too. Something starts to go a little sour and you don't say anything. You think, "They will think I'm petty if I mention it." But if we don't mention it, the next petty thing comes, and by the time you've built up lots of petty things, it's become a huge big thing and you're really angry. You can't deal with all those petty small things because the minute you bring them all up, it's too late to go into all that when it has become a big issue, when it's become so emotionally bound up in your energy that the other person is not listening to you any more.

Confront every situation in the moment and confront every person. If you are feeling something towards them, it is better that you get it out while you're still friends. It's better even if you are enemies already, to face the conflict and have it out with them at the beginning before it gets to blows. That's what you call "creative conflict," because that is the only time conflict can be creative. When you are feeling the feelings, you come out with them; be open and risk your ego, risk getting hammered, risk having your head chopped off, metaphorically, emotionally, psychologically. Because if you don't, it might eventually lead you to get your real head chopped off. That happens, you know. More murders happen in families than from criminals. Statistics show that 50 percent of all murders are committed from emotional frustration among family members. Love soon turns to hatred. Why? Because when they have an argument, the first thing they do is to get the gun. In their emotional rage they don't know themselves, and they shoot their brother or their mother or their father or whoever they think is giving them a hard time. The squabble itself may be over nothing. But the feelings are not nothing. The feelings may have built up from years of frustrations with little things, and eventually the pent up waters flow over the wall of the dam.

If you really want to work on the condition of your consciousness, then you've got to look at the little things which seem petty at the time but are really traces that you leave behind in your mind. Your track record can be seen by looking at how you've come through life, what debris is left behind, what mistakes were there. If your course is zigzag instead of straight, then you have to get your hand on the wheel and start going straight, because if you leave all that debris behind, whether it is emotional relationships with others or whether it is procrastinating and leaving a lot of untied ends loose, eventually it will become a huge impossible situation. You have the choice to leave it all and start all over again from scratch with a new life, or you can cling to the old life and try to patch up the old one. Whichever you choose, you are faced with yourself and your reactions.

So it is best to tackle an issue *now*, whatever it is, even if it is a feeling about another person that springs into your mind at that moment. Rather than going away, confront that person. Say, "This is what I'm feeling. You might not like it, but I'm saying it because I want you to respond to it. Maybe my feeling is not based on any reality. Perhaps I'm misjudging you. Perhaps my assumptions are all screwed up. But I want to get rid of that feeling, somehow, if you will help me." And usually that person will probably point out to you that your feeling is a total misperception.

If somebody eats a meal you've cooked and they don' give you a lot of praise, maybe you think they didn't enjoy it. After several such meals, you might say, "You never seem to enjoy my food. It must be no good." And the person is very shocked and surprised, because they've been enjoying every meal. So they think there is something screwed up in you. "Just because I didn't say I liked it doesn't mean I don't like it." And that gets multiplied throughout the whole of life in almost everything you do, whether it's a thing you do for someone, a kind thought you have for someone, and they don't recognize you've done it or something, and it creates all these funny little feelings. And those all mount up to a state of insecurity in the end. When Christ talks of turning the other cheek, he does not mean that you should be a softie or make pacifism the panacea for all the world's conflicts. He is referring to an attitude of total openness as a way of resolving conflict. If you risk expressing a feeling and somebody confronts you, then instead of reacting or denying what is said, you stay open to the possibility and ask for more clarification (the "other cheek"). Then there is a two-way willingness to share and to settle the conflict. If there is no goodwill between you and your opponent, then, as Christ implies, the willingness on one side alone will not help the situation to resolve itself. This kind of openness may seem like weakness but in fact it is the greatest strength you can have. The more open you are, the bigger a person you will be.

The smaller the person, the more defensive he will be. When he sees another person performing better than he does, instead of going up and saying, "I really like the way you do that. I'd like to be like that myself," and finding out what attitude the successful person has that enables him to be like that, he takes a negative stance and says, "I don't like that because it shows me up. And I don't want to deal with that. I'd rather not be in the presence of that person because he always makes me feel small." And he begins to wallow in self-pity and feel envious. He does not have that feeling of abundance and he doesn't have a good feeling about himself either.

There is a point where you can tell the difference between self-examination and wallowing. It is very important to know that as soon as you feel rotten with yourself, you are not doing something right. You're wallowing. As soon as you begin to cry and feel self-pity, you are injuring yourself spiritually. Self-pity is an indulgence and you are not getting anything out of it but pain, because you're bringing upon yourself a wallowing in negativity. You're allowing that negative thing to take over instead of using it to enhance yourself and saying, "I will put my consciousness into that situation and deal with it." Instead, you say, "Oh, I'm helpless. Poor me. Just look at how everybody else gets everything and I don't," and so forth and so forth.

It's an indulgence to feel lonely. A lonely person is one who is not doing anything about meeting other people or going toward other people, and that person needs to know that. Anyone who is lonely or bored is not making any effort to make friends with anybody. Lonely people are people who refuse to change. They can make the effort any time to go out and radiate, open themselves up and communicate with others, the minute they make up their mind to do it. But if they're going to sit at home and mope, they deserve what they get. They get hell, and they need it.

Pain and suffering and loneliness and frustration and all those things that create disease are only the universe's way of stimulating people to change, or of getting rid of people who are of absolutely no use to the universe, miserable people who have no life in them. Such people are already spiritually dead. They're rigid, and they refuse to change. Lonely people can pick themselves up and find someone if they really have the slightest motivation to share themselves with another person. One other person is all you have to find, not to feel lonely. But you don't even need another person. You can just find your own deeper self, and then you are never lonely, whoever is present, because there is a rich abundance of well-being flowing from you, which is its own reward. You never allow yourself the indulgence to wallow in your own thoughts of self-doubt or fear or insecurity. You never give yourself a chance to fall into that negative space, because you do something right away, *now*, that nips that self-pity in the bud. It is an ego trip to wallow. It's a self-obsessive, narcissist indulgence. The minute you see that and cut it out, you're on your path to success and your life becomes full of challenges that will help you to rise. According to the amount of challenge, so do you rise. Every challenge you master, every challenge you set yourself and master, you rise by that amount of effort you put in.

The Greatest Challenge

Think of your life situation at this moment, whatever it may be, and see if you can turn it into a challenge, so that it becomes an exciting lesson. And the greater challenge that you can make it, to stretch yourself to the utmost, then the greater amount of self-mastery you will have, proportionate to the amount of challenge that you set yourself. If you think about it, you will see that even your own muscles are like that; they grow when you challenge them. This is the natural law, and it is a spiritual law as well. If you set yourself just petty little challenges, then you won't be growing very fast or very high. That is a law of nature, that the greater the challenge you set yourself to master, the greater you will become. And the greater you become, the greater the challenge you will be able to set yourself again. It is a continuous process, but not without some tension. Some people deliberately set themselves the challenge to do something impossible, something never done before in the history of mankind. They do this because to do ordinary things that are done every day represents no challenge. Right now it is impossible for even great nations with billions of dollars to harness the sun's energy economically. It is impossible for them to feed the hungry millions of the world. How can any single individual tackle such huge problems? The answer is that governments will never tackle them without some individual making a breakthrough or achieving the solution first. Every world problem is an individual opportunity rather than an impossibility.

How do you find the balance between setting great challenges and asking too much of yourself, beyond your capacity? You have to look at your situation, because it is different for everyone. You could think of what the greatest challenge is for you right now, but if you confide this challenge to a friend, they may say it is no challenge at all, because everybody's challenge is special to him or to her, and what's difficult for you may be easy for the next person. For one person it may be difficult to save money; for another person it may be difficult to spend money. Some people have a problem of always falling in love. It's usually the wrong person but they're always very quick to fall in love and give their heart away. And the easier they give their heart away, the more people will walk all over it and use it as a doormat. But the problem for other people is that they can't give their heart away because they can't find anyone that they can trust enough to give it to. So they're very miserly with themselves and find it very hard indeed to fall in love, because there is always something restraining them from trusting their heart to someone else. This is no small problem because it is worldwide and leads to world conflicts.

Every problem you think is the ultimate challenge for you, could maybe be done in five minutes flat by most other people. If you read Shakespeare's plays, every character, particularly in the tragedies, is given a situation which is almost impossible for him to handle. Everyone in the play has a particular problem. They all find it very easy to handle the other person's problem, but not their own. That problem is called "the tragic flaw." In all great drama and particularly Shakespeare, there is a tragic flaw. And that is what

I am talking about when I talk about challenge. Where is your Achilles' heel? Where does the snake bite you? That's what you have to find out. Where the snake bites one person will be a different place than where it bites another. Some people get bitten in their pockets; some people get bitten in other places. But the snake, when it bites, has a pretty good aim for the most vulnerable spot.

All this has nothing to do with anyone else. If you probe deep enough into the inner world of a person, you'll find that very few people have the exact same problems. There aren't any problems, in fact; the only problems are people. They are given certain challenges. Life at any given moment is a challenge. Even if you don't have any problems, that itself is a challenge. To sit under a redwood tree for the rest of your life and be in bliss is a problem, because for you just selfishly to have bliss all for yourself and see the rest of the world in misery is an enormous problem, isn't it? To be blissed out so that you don't have to pay any attention to what's happening on this planet is a challenge, because what did you come to this world for, anyway? What use are you in this whole universe if you've got bliss and nobody else has it? If you have love and nobody else has it? So your problem becomes how to give your bliss or love away. Do you go around tapping people on the head? "Do you want bliss? Do you want bliss? Do you want bliss?" They say, "No, I want my problem." And that is a challenge.

DOING YOUR BEST

Disciplining one's own consciousness, one's own mind, one's own appetites, and becoming master over the wanderings of one's good intentions, is much more difficult than just doing whatever we are told to do. And so it is obvious that any person who has a naturally indulgent nature, is going to have more problems than those who love discipline. An undisciplined mind or an undisciplined person is a real rebel when it comes to self-mastery, because discipline is an unaccustomed state. They're used to doing just what they please. Once you can find the secret of how much power it gives you over yourself when you can discipline your mind or your emotions or your appetites, you will know how rewarding this self-discipline is. This kind of self-control of our own mental state can only be achieved by deep meditation practiced on a regular basis. It is the same if we are going to become an Olympic athlete because the physical laws of the universe are no different from spiritual laws. You must meditate with the same intensity as an athlete. You don't get results unless you are aware of what you have to put into it. If you only put half into it, you only get half back. And half a result is not very rewarding. It's like doing something half-baked. Even if you put three-quarters in and get three-quarters back, the other quarter you're always missing, and that is the quarter that you need to make your discipline truly fulfilling and not just a grind.

One way to get self-discipline is to imitate those who are good at it, those who are getting results. Find a model. If you find it difficult to be disciplined, try to find out what motivates those people who do like discipline. Ask those people, search the minds of those people who are good at it. Get into their world and come out of your own little world. If you are so obsessed with what you're *not* getting, with how everything affects you, with how you feel about things, you miss 90 percent of what is really going on around you. Under your very nose are answers you never see! So the secret is to forget the self-obsession and try to get inside the worlds of others and see just what motivates them to do things outside themselves, selfless things. The more you work in a selfless way, the less self-obsession you have, until your self-regarding instinct eventually goes away altogether.

You can't just get rid of this self-regarding sentiment overnight; it's going to be quite a time before you switch around from being what you've been taught to be, which is to go out to get things for yourself, get money, get power, climb socially, elbow your way up through society, become somebody, all that sort of stuff which leads you to be thinking of yourself as a competitive being. Such self-obsession will never get you any happiness. You might own lots of things, a nice swimming pool, a nice house, a Rolls Royce, but you'll never be happy that way, because it is impossible to be happy while being selfish. If you live your life for others, and if you think of others, happiness will come to you, because in the doing for others, you'll receive far more and you'll never lack anything. You'll never lack money, you'll never lack friends, you'll never lack love. And you will never lack that feeling of always being filled full.

If you do your best, you can't do any more, and you are fulfilled. So you never worry about whether or not someone else is ahead of you. But if you always hold something back to keep it for yourself and you don't do your best, and you are possessive about your life and your love, there is always something missing in your own feeling. If you don't let it all hang out and give your whole self, there is never a feeling of complete reward, a psychic income which comes like a message from within you and says, "You know you did your best. You can't do any more." If you know you've done that, you don't worry that others are more skilled than you or that they compete more aggressively than you, because you are unique. Everyone is unique. And everyone has got different skills to offer the world. The world is like an oyster, you must pry it open to find the hidden pearl of high price. But if you don't open the oyster you never get the pearl even though you have the oyster, so you never enjoy it. To open the oyster requires skill in loving the world even if you are not sure your best is really enough. But if you do your best, you'll always have that feeling that you've got your niche, that destiny places you just where you are to unfold your potential.

If you have that awareness or caring for others, if you are loving, that is your reward, because you experience that love. That very love that flows out from you turns you on. A person in love is always surrounded by friends, because people can feel it. You don't have to be a star performer. If you are filled with that love, the love itself is its own reward. It absolutely gets rid of that self-obsession which is always worrying, "How do I look? I didn't get a present; they got a present," all the time comparing when there is no need to compare. If you're filled with love, you don't need anyone else to tell you that you're okay. You're not looking for someone else to confirm you all the time, and you're not worried about who sees what work you do, because the recognition is not coming from outside. It's coming from within, inside your own mind, saying, "I am well pleased with you. You are doing your best, and even if nobody else ever sees it, I see it and I know what is in your heart."

I have proved this in my own life countless times by doing some task I did not really want to do but knew no one else wanted to do it either. By deliberately approaching what is difficult and doing my best while leaving the results up to a higher order of intelligence, I have found that that intelligence never lets me down. Even when I am wrong and take risks no one wants to take, I know that my sense of conviction that everything happens for good in the end, has a vital part to play in attracting this higher intelligence into my life experience. I also know that if I don't do my best with what intelligence I do have, I will not be given any more.

So you see this is cosmic law operating here in a very simple way which manifests in a complex and inscrutable wisdom. That wisdom is the sharpest tool by which you can know yourself and it comes only to those who can persist to the end in doing the hardest work there is on the planet.

That work is to conquer your self-obsession.

NURTURING THE HERO WITHIN YOU

Success is a way of life, but what can inspire the reader of these chapters to want to undertake the hardest work there is on the planet, namely self-mastery? You can conquer the financial worlds, you can conquer the world of fame, or you can conquer the world by force, but it is more difficult to conquer your self than to conquer the whole world. The thread which leads through all these chapters is the same thread which led the hero Theseus back through the maze of life to amaze those who awaited his victory over the Minotaur—the bull which represented the earthly powers.

Heroes differ from the average person only in their commitment to overcome their fears and to stay the distance. They begin to change themselves step by step by working on their own patterns of consciousness. Today a large number of people must begin to do this or the whole world is headed for trouble. The entire social fabric can only be changed when individual lives are changed. But without a motive, who will try? Without the inner drive to succeed, who will risk? Without the feeling that you can personally benefit from becoming all-giving, who will be selfless?

Success is not only financial success but also success in the higher sense. Success is not just a higher spiritual level but also a mastery of worldliness too, for to be great on one level alone is not the success of the whole. This makes the difference between the selfish person and the saint. The saint works to uplift the whole and is committed to the whole truth. Financial success by itself can be achieved at the expense of the truth.

Truth and success are ultimately one, because we cannot use the wrong means to reach the right goal. There is no truthful way we can unravel the fabric of our lives by consistently ignoring what we have done in the past. Our past will always catch up with us in time. And what we think now in the present moment about what we have done in the past, will determine the way we can change the future.

To be inspired to change the future means we must live in the dream of the future but act in the now while the future is still yet unmade, for once the future moment becomes the present and passes into the past, it is but a memory. The living now is the key to achieving success for the whole, because any life well lived in this moment inherits the kingdom of heaven and becomes a blessing upon us all.

If you who read these few words can dig deep in the rich compost of your inner garden, the flower of the self can blossom in self-mastery. And the seeds of that flower shall have the power to replicate themselves throughout the world.